Written by Best-Selling Authors

Dr. Darren R. Weissman
and B.T. Brunelle

THE DAILY LESSONS of
INFINITE LOVE & GRATITUDE

The power of a positive attitude
can lift the world and make you feel really good!

Illustrated by George Milo Buck

Written by Dr. Darren R. Weissman and B.T. Brunelle

Illustrated by George Milo Buck

Co-editing and production by Jon Brunelle

Additional production by Mary Gustafson

Printed by Create Space 2012

ISBN: 1475047673

ISBN-13: 9781475047677

OUR DEDICATIONS

FROM DARREN

This book is dedicated to my 3 angels from heaven, Joya Ruth, Rumi Neve, and Liam Yale.
With Infinite Love & Gratitude,
Daddy

FROM BAHIA

I would like to express my deepest appreciation to my beloved Mother, Father and Brother for giving me my first experiences of the power of love and a positive attitude.
Bahia

· · ·

And to all of you young and not so young readers, who are taking this present moment to explore these daily lessons, we say...
Thank You and Enjoy!

INTRODUCTION

We're so excited that you're holding this book! Your dreams and imagination create a magical doorway to the future. This book was inspired from dreams, imagination, and intention to live in a peaceful world. It is with the deepest respect and honor that Bahia and I have co-created our imaginings into a reality. The future holds the promise of the thoughts that are creating it. The intention of Infinite Love & Gratitude is to inspire and awaken you to simple and powerful ways to feel really good in your life.

I first awoke to the power of Infinite Love & Gratitude in 2002. Ever since, I've been travelling around the world teaching and sharing this incredible LifeLine. I'm deeply humbled and grateful to be able to make such a direct impact. Like a seed awakening to life, the power for you to thrive comes from within. Infinite Love & Gratitude is an exciting journey of growing through life's experiences.

The 20 Lessons and Spotlights in this book are designed to create a roadmap for understanding and transforming negative ways of thinking into positive and empowering ways of living. As much as this is illustrated for children, the lessons are for everyone and applicable for the inner child within each and every one of us. To our children's future and the future of humanity . . . This book is dedicated to you!

Keep shining bright!

With Infinite Love & Gratitude~

Dr. Darren R. Weissman & Bahia T. Brunelle

HERE'S WHAT'S INSIDE

PART ONE

---

20 Fun Daily Lessons
Of Infinite Love and Gratitude

The stage has been set for the show to begin
With colorful pictures and rhymes that sing,
Starring Infinite Love and Gratitude
And The Power of a Positive Attitude.
Hold onto your seats, there's excitement ahead,
20 fun daily lessons that are meant to be read.
You can read them at school, you can read them at home.
They will make you feel great, when you make them your own!

Lesson One

Your Magic Wands

Positive words are like magic wands,
Sending good vibrations that go on and on.
They make people happy all around.
You can reach the whole world with one loving sound.

Think about how it makes you smile
When the words "I Love You" travel miles and miles,
Coming through your phone or radio dial
From a friendly grown-up or a friendly child!

THE GOLDEN ROAD

Be positive, be confident.
The time you take for yourself is time well spent.
Slow down and relax if you're feeling tense.
Give yourself a hug and some compliments.

Being positive gets a big A-Plus.
It moves you forward like a yellow school bus.
Ride on a road that you can trust,
One that's paved in gold and magic pixie dust!

FOCUS ON WHAT YOU LOVE

Negative words are like sour grapes.
They make you want to cover your ears with sticky tape.
Everything they touch gets bent out of shape.
The second you hear them you'd like to escape.

Think about how it makes you sad,
How words like "stupid" sound so bad.
Focus on the things that make you glad,
What you love to do and all the fun you've had!

WINNING THE RACE

You can still have fun when the sky is gray.
Let the sunshine clear the clouds away.
Follow your heart and it will show you the way.
In all kinds of weather have a wonderful day.

Being negative gets a Minus Sign.
It can weaken your body and cloud your mind.
In a marathon race, you can fall behind.
What makes you a winner is being kind!

YOU ARE A WIZARD

Powerful words are what wizards use
To cast a spell or make your dreams come true.
When it comes to words you have the power to choose.
Abracadabra you're a wizard too!

Now let's take a look at some powerful words,
Ones that you've probably already heard.
They can help you feel confident and reassured,
Make a seagull soar and a kitten purr!

Lesson Six

Positive and Powerful Words

The word Infinite means without an end
Like a comet that keeps coming round again,
The way friends will be forever friends
And kids will always like to pretend.

Love is what you feel in your heart.
It keeps us together when we're apart.
It blooms with the flowers in your yard.
And flows from the strings of your guitar.

13

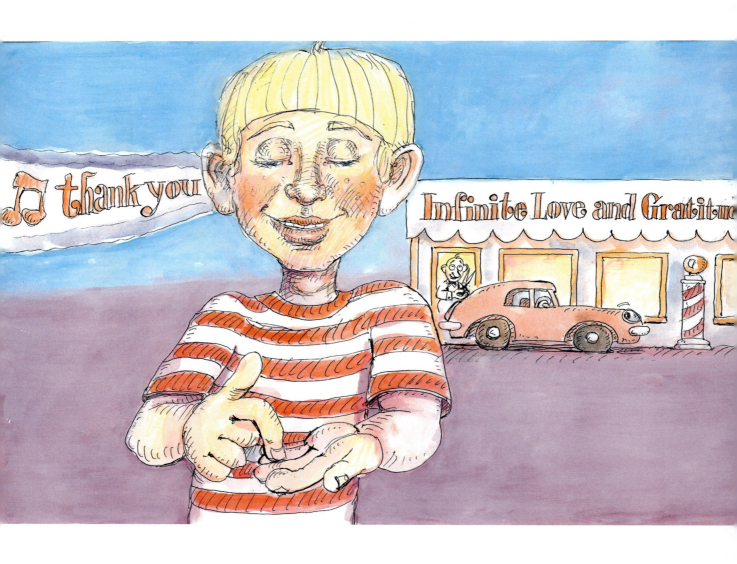

Music to Our Ears

The word Gratitude is really great to hear.
Every "Thank You" is music to our ears.
It's being grateful for what we hold dear,
Counting our blessings as they appear.

What gives you a healthy attitude
Is to feel appreciation for all you're going through.
So open your heart to its fullest magnitude
By saying out loud Infinite Love & Gratitude!

Your Body Can Talk

Humans have been talking for a long, long time,
Turning sounds into words full of rhythm and rhyme.
Some are loud as thunder, some are quiet as chimes.
Words motivate you when there are mountains to climb.

Before there were words folks could understand
They spoke with their bodies, faces, and hands,
Universal signs and sounds from each land
Like laughter and crying and the language of dance.

THE LOVING HANDS GAME

Why don't we play a game that's fun to share,
Talk with our fingers to show how much we care.
Hold your 2 hands way up in the air
Like a high five that people do everywhere.

Lift your index fingers, thumbs and pinkies up.
Fold your ring and middle fingers down like a cup.
You'll be sending out a message of love
With the peace and beauty that comes from above.

RICH WITH LOVE

This hand gesture can go wherever you go.
There are countless ways for your love to be shown.
One candle can make another one glow.
It's a beautiful light that will grow and grow.

If you want to give love to someone else,
First you have to give some to yourself.
Love leads the way to optimal health
And health, not money, is our greatest wealth.

THE 5 BASICS

There are 5 Basic Steps to staying healthy and strong.
Follow them daily, and you can't go wrong.
They're as easy as singing your favorite song.
If you're ready to hear them, just bang a gong!

Water and food are high on the list.
Exercise and rest bring circulation and bliss.
The right quantity, quality and frequency is
Very important, and remember this…

A SHINING STAR

Own your power, you're a powerful one.
There is nobody like you under the sun.
So full of wisdom even though you are young,
You've accomplished things only you could have done.

Life is a party you can't rehearse.
Some balloons will rise while others may burst.
Be a friend to yourself for better or worse.
You're a shining star in the universe!

Lesson Thirteen

YOUR AMAZING BODY

Check out your body, it's an amazing machine
With organs and glands that are busy building,
Consuming, digesting, and eliminating,
Thinking, planning, and remembering.

Treat it like a castle with love and respect.
Good things to eat and drink have a great effect.
It's so cool how we're different like the cards in a deck
Every body is beautiful, unique and perfect!

BELIEVE IN YOURSELF

If your tummy aches and you feel kind of sick
From too much ice cream with portions too big,
Tell your Mom and Dad, see what advice they give.
Say some positive words to help yourself quick.

It may take some rest when your heart needs fueling
Or drinking a glass of water can be really soothing.
Maybe a walk to get your muscles moving,
Most of all, believe you'll get well and soon you'll be grooving!

Colorful Changes

Positive words can make you feel great.
Picture each letter, some have curves, some are straight.
Listen to the colorful sounds they make.
The ones filled with love are too bright for hate.

Think about something you'd like to change.
Is there a part of your health or life that feels strange?
Say Infinite Love and see what you gain.
Add some Gratitude and you're well on your way!

Lesson Sixteen

YOUR ENERGY

Every form of life has energy,
All the people, plants and animals you see,
The mountains, valleys, oceans, and streams,
It's the golden thread that connects you and me.

Negative thoughts divide us with walls.
They drain our energy and cause our spirits to fall.
Positive thoughts unite us all,
When we're working together or just having a ball!

OCEANS OF EMOTIONS

Did you know that your body's a lot like the earth,
Made mostly of water that rises and swirls.
And water's affected by sounds and by words.
The health of water affects all boys and girls.

Your emotions change like a winding river,
Like a roller coaster ride that makes you laugh or shiver.
If you're mad, glad, scared, want to cry or quiver
Then talk about it, get it out, let your thoughts be delivered!

Lesson Eighteen

YOU ARE CREATIVE

Creativity is inside every soul.
Everyone has ambitions, dreams, and goals.
What do you create that makes you feel whole?
Do you love to invent and watch what unfolds?

Can your creations set your mind at ease,
Like you're floating on a raft as calm as can be?
Inside everyone's heart is a spark of peace
Shining light on the shadows and setting spirits free!

Lesson Nineteen

LESSONS ARE GIFTS

Learn from the earth and learn from the moon.
Write your own song and sing your own tune.
You have your own orbit that belongs to just you.
You're starting a life that's shiny and new.

Keep working your magic each day that you live.
In every challenge find the gift that it gives.
Each kid is a hero and all heroes were kids.
You're a piece of the puzzle in a world where you fit!

Lesson Twenty

INFINITE YOU

Look in the mirror each morning when you rise.
Your infinite possibilities are there in your eyes.
Treasure this moment as one more prize.
Keep on smiling till everything shines.

Imagine something that you would like to do.
What is a dream that you intend to come true?
You can make miracles, it's all up to you.
Say Infinite Love & Gratitude!

PART TWO

The Spotlight's On You!

Now it's your turn to be the star of the show,
To ask any questions and share what you know.
Discussions are a great way to learn something new
And everyone has their unique point of view.
So step up onstage for your song and dance.
Express yourself, here's a wonderful chance.
You have great things to say and great things to do.
Please share what these lessons mean to you!

THE SPOTLIGHT'S ON YOU!

Now that we have covered 20 Infinite Love & Gratitude Lessons,
let's hear what you have to say.

One: Your Magic Wands

Did you know that your words are like magic? You can make yourself and others feel good or bad, happy or sad, peaceful or mad, simply with what you say. What does the word "Positive" mean to you?

For some people, this word means optimistic, constructive, helpful, encouraging, affirmative, up and upbeat. Can you come up with examples of words that are positive? What are some of your favorites?

Do they give you feelings that you can describe?

Action Step: Go share your positive words with someone else, and observe how it makes you and the other person feel.

Two: The Golden Road

How does your day go when you are feeling positive about yourself? Does it seem easier to accomplish your goals? Do you feel like things are going your way instead of getting in your way? Do you ever stop to give yourself and others some encouraging words? What are the kinds of the things that you might say?

Action Step: Smile at people for no other reason than simply to share your smile. Say "Hi!" to people at school, in a grocery store, or while in a restaurant. Do other people smile back and say "Hi!" to you? How does it make you feel?

Three: Focus On What You Love

There may have been moments in your life when people have said negative things that you did not want to hear. Has this ever stopped you from having a good time? If and when you find yourself being affected by a person or a situation that is unpleasant, here is a key to how you can stay on a positive course.

Action Step: Do your best to focus on the things that you love about yourself and the world. This could include your many talents and skills, your family, friends and pets, the games that you like to play, the subjects in school that you enjoy, the beautiful places which you have visited, and the joyful sounds of music, singing and celebration. Notice that when you have a positive focus, negative experiences can instantly begin to change. Now go on and have a great time doing what is meaningful for you!

Four: Winning The Race

In a race, winning is not necessarily about finishing first. What scores you the highest points is your positive attitude, and how much you can enjoy the thrill of running, swimming, cycling, etc. Were you ever on a team in a relay race? Did you have so much fun that you felt like a winner even before the race was over? You become an automatic success when you enjoy the process of doing something.

Negative thoughts, words and actions can make you feel weak all over. If you want to be strong, put your best foot forward by supporting yourself and others. That way, everyone gets to be a winner!

Action Step: Next time you're playing a team game such as soccer, basketball, tennis or tag, cheer for the other people that you're playing with. Regardless of which team is winning, support everyone to have fun and do their very best. Pay attention to how much fun everyone has when you support each other.

Five: You Are A Wizard

Would you rather cast spells or make dreams come true? Positive thoughts and words are the stuff that dreams are made of. And guess what, you have the power to pick and choose the words you use and the things you do. What dreams would you like to make come true? Pick up your magic wand, and imagine yourself being who you'd like to be, and going where you'd like to go. See yourself living the life you dream of, and you're already halfway there!

Action Step: At the beginning and end of your day, while still in your bed, concentrate on your dreams. Imagine yourself living your dreams. See yourself as if you're already there, picturing yourself healthy and happy. Do this every day, and notice how the power of positive intention and imagination can impact the health of your body and your relationships.

Six: Positive And Powerful Words

What do the words "Infinite" and "Love" mean to you? Infinite is a big word. It's as big as what it means.

When something is infinite, it is endless, like the sky and like time. It has no limits, and it can't even be measured. What are some things that you think are infinite? Have you ever thought about what the word "Love" means? Is it an emotion of strong affection? Do you love anyone so much that it can't be measured? What if you felt that way about everyone, including yourself? What if everybody felt that way about everyone?

Action Step: In situations where you feel stuck and are unsure of what to do, open your heart to the power of love and the infinite part of you. Know that love is the one thing that heals everything, and begin to think, feel, speak, and act with love. Start a journal, and write down how it feels to face challenges in this way.

Seven: Music To Our Ears

We all have words that make us feel good when we hear them. Oftentimes it also gives us joy to say these very same words. What are words that you like to hear? Think of how it make you feel warm and happy inside when someone says, "Thank You Very Much," or "Please," or "You're welcome."

Action Step: What are some words that are music to your ears? Make a commitment to yourself each day to say, "Thank you!" when someone does something nice for you; or "Please" when you would like something from someone else; and say, "You're welcome" when a person expresses appreciation for your acts of kindness.

Eight: Your Body Can Talk

Before humans came up with the bright idea of creating words, they used lots of body language and vocal sounds to communicate. To say what was on their minds, they moved different parts of their bodies, while making grunting, groaning, growling, gasping, and gleeful noises. People today still talk with their bodies, when words alone just aren't enough. They roll their eyes, wrinkle their noses, smile and frown, nod, shake their heads, shrug their shoulders, cross their fingers, wave hello and goodbye, click their heels, dance and jump for joy! What are some ways in which you talk with your body?

Action Step: Pay attention to how your friends and family express themselves without saying any words. See if you can express your feelings with facial expressions and movements of your body.

Nine: The Loving Hands Game

Sign language goes on all around us. Every day you can see children and adults using it to express themselves. It's a way that people who have trouble hearing can still be actively learning, teaching, and sharing their valuable thoughts and ideas. If you go to a ball game, you can see coaches, referees and athletes using it. If you go to a concert, you can see the conductor waving a baton and using hand gestures to direct the musicians. What are some other forms of sign language that you see and use in your daily life?

Action Step: Now you can add The Loving Hands Gesture as a new and fun way of saying "I Love You" and "Infinite Love & Gratitude." Hold your hand in the "I Love You" sign posture and say "Infinite Love & Gratitude" to your friends, family, and parts of your body that are feeling sad or hurt. Notice how it makes you and them feel.

Ten: Rich With Love

What are the most important and valuable things to you? Did you know that you are like a treasure chest? The infinite love that comes from your heart is more precious than all of the gold coins in the whole wide world. You will have the opportunity throughout your life to create work for yourself that generates an abundance of wealth and satisfaction. Please remember this, that while money, toys and other material stuff can be fun and useful, your greatest wealth will always be the love that you already have. It is this love that will bring you good health and happiness. And all the love that you give to others will come back to you like a fountain that keeps getting bigger and more beautiful!

Action Step: Every day take time to write in your journal 5 things that you're grateful for. Share your gratitude by saying, "Thank you!" and telling others that you appreciate having them in your life.

Eleven: The 5 Basics

Are you ready to review The 5 Basics? These are five things you can do every day to be healthy and stay healthy. They're as easy as pie to remember, but you have to do more than just remember them. Do them well and they'll do you well! Pay attention to getting the right quantity and quality of each one. Find out what the proper balance is for you. Eat good nutritious food. Drink plenty of water. Get adequate rest. Exercise and do your best to do it where you can breathe clean fresh air. And last but not least, own your power. This isn't about having power over others. It's about expressing yourself, and recognizing the infinite power that exists in you and in everyone to think good thoughts and to do great things. Are you already doing the 5 Basics?

Action Step: Begin today by following The 5 Basics for Optimal Health. Exchange soda pop for fresh juice and plenty of pure water; eat fruits, vegetables and proteins rather than sugar; play and exercise, rather than be sitting on a couch all day, watching television and playing video games; be sure to get rest for both your body and mind; and most of all, embrace each and every moment with Infinite Love & Gratitude.

Twelve: A Shining Star

The way to have friends is to be a friend. Before you can be a friend to others, you need to first be a friend to yourself. Life has its ups and downs. You will have good days, and not-so-good days. What all days have in common is that each one of them teaches you something. On days when your balloons and kites don't fly, and things don't seem to be going the way you planned, what do you do? Do you blame yourself or someone else? Or do you look back on all of the times when you have solved problems and handled difficult situations with everything turning out just fine?

Action Step: Remember to always be a friend to yourself, and you'll keep shining bright! Talking to a parent, teacher, and good friend will help you to gain a new perspective. We know that when we change the way we view things, the things that we're viewing begin to change.

Thirteen: Your Amazing Body

Anatomy books are fascinating to look at. They are full of glossy rainbow colored pictures of what the human body looks like inside and out. Would you like to know more about your body? What parts of it interest you the most? Would you like to learn the names of all the different bones, how the brain works, what keeps your heart pumping and the jobs that are done by each of your organs? How are all bodies alike? In what ways can they be different? Your amazing body is taking care of you. Do you take care of your body by giving it The 5 Basics every day? Remember that when you think good thoughts, you are taking care of your body and your mind, because they work together.

Action Step: Tell your body how much you love it. Look in the mirror and say, "Thank you body, I love you. Thank you body, you are loved. Thank you body, you are pure love!" Do this every day, and you'll soon notice that your body speaks back to you with feelings of confidence, more energy, and greater strength in every way!

Fourteen: Believe In Yourself

Being kind and understanding to others, especially when they are not feeling well, accomplishes two things. It makes them feel better, and it makes you feel good inside. It can help to restore their faith in themselves. It can also remind you to believe in yourself and the power that you have to make things better for everyone. In the same way that you can help someone else, you can also talk to yourself when you are the one who is not feeling well. Maybe you have a sore throat; or you bruised your knee; or someone hurt your feelings; or you had a bad dream. Talking about what's going on will bring it out of the darkness and into the light. Don't be afraid to ask for help. That's what your parents, teachers, doctors and friends are for. What have you done before that helped to make things better for you? Did you think positive thoughts, and say positive words? Did you believe in yourself?

Action Step: Today, focus on one or more friends, who are feeling stress in their bodies or in their relationships. Teach them the "I Love You" hand sign and Infinite Love & Gratitude.

Notice how it lifts them up. When you're having a tough day and feeling down, make it a priority to focus on the positive aspect of things and notice how fast you start to feel the positive shift in your heart.

Fifteen: Colorful Changes

The only thing in life that doesn't change is change itself. It is a part of our everyday lives. The more we can appreciate how much we learn and grow from these changes, the happier we will be. There are changes that we welcome, like when a caterpillar turns into a brilliantly colored butterfly, and when winter turns into spring and all the fruit trees are bursting with pink and white blossoms. And then there are changes that can make us fearful or sad, like when lightning strikes, or when a close friend moves far away to another town. It helps to welcome these unknown and unexpected events. Think of them as coming attractions and adventures that you can look forward to, like a surprise birthday party or a new vacation spot that you are visiting for the first time.

Action Step: Have you noticed any changes in yourself lately? Is your hair longer? Are you getting stronger? What changes have you made? What changes can you make . . . maybe taking a new route to school, rearranging the furniture in your room, or changing your mind about something? What else? What do you notice when you deliberately change the way you move through life, and intentionally change how life moves through you?

Sixteen: Your Energy

Scientists have discovered that everyone and every living thing in the universe has energy. Since the universe consists of more than just our planet Earth, that means we're all part of one big family! What are some things that give us a feeling of togetherness? Is positive energy one of them?

How do negative thoughts affect your energy? What about positive thoughts? What kinds of things do you do to keep your energy strong and your spirits high? Do you eat a healthy snack? Do you visit the park and play on the merry-go-round, the Jungle Jim, the swings and the slides? How about reading a good book, telling a funny joke and laughing with some jovial friends?

Action Step: Rub your hands together really quickly for 10 seconds. Now place your hands apart from each other as if you were holding an energy ball. Slowly bring your hands closer and then farther away from each other, while making sure your hands don't touch. Notice that you begin to feel a tingly energy on your palms. You're feeling your energy! Now focus your energy in a healthy way with positive thoughts, happy feelings, and kind words. This is a powerful exercise to practice every day.

Seventeen: Oceans Of Emotions

You have a mind, body, spirit and emotions. There are no good or bad emotions. Each one of them exists for a reason. Everyone has experienced Anger, Fear, Joy, Sorrow, Worry, Sympathy and Love. Learning how to balance these emotions will help you to lead a happy and harmonious life. Maintaining a balance is a constant process that can be enjoyed. You are doing it when you express your emotions in a positive and constructive way to someone who cares. Who do you talk to when you need to get something off your chest? To your family? To your friends? To your pets? Who else?

Action Step: Talk to the person inside of you by saying things like, "I'm going to go for a run and blow off some steam;" or "The nervousness and fear that I am feeling will soon pass, and I'll be able to sing my heart out for this audience;" or "I feel so great that I'm going to paint a picture that will make others happy too!"

Getting in touch with your emotions means that you are paying attention to what your feelings are telling you. Be true to yourself, and that's the way to be!

Eighteen: You Are Creative

Everyone is full of creativity. To be creative means that you have original ideas and special abilities that belong to only you. It's when you go deep inside the well of your

mind and imagination to draw out thoughts that no one else has ever had. Have you ever made up a story and acted it out? Do poems and melodies come to you that you never heard before? Think of all the times that you have created something from nothing. How often have you stretched beyond the usual and predictable way of doing things? Did you ever bake a cake and add a few ingredients that weren't in the recipe? Have you ever carved a pumpkin, designed a costume, planned a science project, built sand castles and snow men?

World famous rock stars, award winning actors and ingenious inventors are all creative. So are your neighbors next door, and so are you!

Action Step: Ignite the creative genius within by learning something new, and creating something new. Choose to learn a new musical instrument, language, or other form of self-expression, like painting or writing a story. Life is filled with infinite possibilities, and we may never know our greatest passions unless we are open to new creative adventures.

Nineteen: Lessons Are Gifts

From when we are young to when we grow old, we are learning lessons. Many of them are fun to learn, while others can be very challenging. At times it may take a great deal of strength, patience and faith for us to be able to see through the strange wrapping paper that covers some of these lessons.

What are examples of lessons that were fun for you to learn? Did you learn them at school, on a field trip, at a museum or at home? Where else? What were the times when a mistake, an embarrassing situation, or an unexpected event turned out all right in the end? Did you learn a valuable lesson as well? Have you ever trained a dog to do tricks, taught someone how to tie their shoelaces, helped your classmates with their homework, or shown a friend how to pitch a baseball? Have you ever made it easier for another person to understand how to do something? If the answer is Yes to any of these questions, Congratulations! You are a teacher as well as a student!

As we travel down life's highway, there are many road signs that we can follow. One that guarantees infinite miles of satisfaction says, "Yearn To Learn, Strive To Thrive, and Know You'll Grow!"

Action Step: Make it a point to teach friends things that they would like to know how to do. Teach them how to whistle, spin a hula-hoop, or ride a bicycle. Stick with it until they get it. You will all be filled with so much gratitude that you shared the journey of a new adventure!

Twenty: Infinite You

Your possibilities are as unlimited as the universe itself. Start off each day by asking yourself this question… "What is possible for me?" See what answers you get. If you really listen, you will hear your own wise voice answering. It may say things like, "I have my whole life ahead of me. I can do anything I set my mind to. Nothing can stop me. The sky's the limit!" Then ask, "What else is possible?" and watch how the answers keep coming. If you make peace with yourself, if you are persistent, and if you maintain a positive attitude, you will be amazed by how much you can do.

Life offers a banquet of opportunities. And we are powerful beings who can make sensible choices. Do your best to see beyond the perceived limitations of a moment. Be careful of falling into that trap. Instead, take responsibility for your decisions, and replace doubt with determination. Handle your worries and fears with communication, and forgive yourself for having them. Whether or not you have trophies, medals and awards, you are a champion. Do your best to not let praise or criticism from others govern your self-esteem. Give yourself the rewards and encouragement that will help you to accomplish your goals.

The future is like a yummy ice cream sundae that we're so excited to dive into. The past is a meal that we remember. What is ready to be enjoyed is the plate of food that's in front of us right now.

Action Step: Today, what do you have that you appreciate? What are some things you have done that you are proud of? What would you like to give to this world, and what would you like to receive?

Remember that life is an abundant feast that is always available to you.

Your possibilities and you are infinite!

MEET THE AUTHORS
AND ILLUSTRATOR

Dr. Darren R. Weissman is an internationally renowned physician, speaker, educator, developer of The LifeLine Technique®, and best-selling author. Darren and his wife Sarit are conscious parents of their three children, Joya, Rumi, and Liam. Darren's passion is to inspire and empower others with the power of Infinite Love & Gratitude. You can hear Darren on his weekly radio show, The Heart of the Matter on www.hayhouseradio.com. To find out more please visit www.drdarrenweissman.com.

B.T. Brunelle, aka Bahia T. Brunelle, is a widely acclaimed author, musician and educator. Residing with her family on the Pacific Coast of the United States, she writes books of fiction and non-fiction for readers of all ages. Her writing reflects the same spirit of optimism that goes into her volunteer work with non-profit environmental and humanitarian groups. She says, "As a writer and teacher, I deeply appreciate the value of Dr. Weissman's enlightening and empowering messages for adults and children. It is very exciting and fulfilling to be a part of this **Infinite Love and Gratitude** book!"

George Milo Buck has lived and studied throughout the United States, Europe and Africa. He earned a Bachelor of Arts degree from San Jose State University. Schooled in "The Old Masters" tradition, he works in watercolors, and oils on canvas. George has been an art director and illustrator for projects like the Oscar nominated motion picture "The Situation." He also works as a portrait artist and teacher.

Manufactured by Amazon.ca
Bolton, ON